Merry Christmas

To:

From:

a
CINCINNATI
Night Before
christmas

Written by
Nadine Woodard Huffman

Illustrated by
Marilyn M. Lebhar

Based on the poem by Clement C. Moore

ORANGE *frazer* PRESS
Wilmington, Ohio

ISBN 978-1933197-845
Copyright©2011 Cincinnati Bright Hope, LLC

Published for Cincinnati Bright Hope, LLC by:
Orange Frazer Press
P.O. Box 214
Wilmington, OH 45177
Telephone 1.800.852.9332 for price and shipping information.
Websites: *www.orangefrazercustombooks.com* or *www.orangefrazer.com*

BENGALS, BUSKEN BAKERY, CROSLEY, GRAETER'S and the GRAETER'S logo, LaROSA'S PIZZERIA, MACY'S, MONTGOMERY INN and MONTGOMERY INN WORLD FAMOUS RIBS KING, and REDS are trademarks of their respective owners and are used with permission. Krohn Conservatory, Nativity Crib, Union Terminal, Holiday Junction, Cincinnati Zoo and Botanical Garden, Festival of Lights, and Cincinnati Ballet are named with permission.

"Bootsy," "Kunzel," and "Nuxie" are used with the gracious permission of their respective families.

The beliefs expressed herein are those of the author and illustrator, and do not necessarily represent the views of the trademark owners, organizations, and families named in the book, or Orange Frazer Press.
Scripture quotations are taken from the *Holy Bible*, New Living Translation, copyright©1996. Used by permission of Tyndale House Publishers, Inc., Wheaton, Illinois 60189. All rights reserved.

Watercolor paints were used for the full color art.
Artwork scanned digitally by Robin Imaging Services.
Book and cover design: Chad DeBoard, Orange Frazer Press
Author and illustrator photographs: Kristin Moser Photography

All proceeds from this book support Greater Cincinnati not-for-profit adoption organizations. For more information visit our site:
www.CincinnatiNightBeforeChristmas.com

Library of Congress Control Number: 2011930578

Third printing, 2013
Printed in China
May 6, 2013
Plant & Location: Printed by Everbest Printing (Guangzhou, China), Co. Ltd
111239

To all the adopted children who have
touched our hearts,
To the generous people of Cincinnati,
And to our beloved families.

N.W.H. and M.M.L.

'Twas the night before Christmas here in Cincinnati,
Where our story begins with a young boy named Matty.

M A T

POP

He had just gotten up from
a short winter's nap,

And was all snuggled up on
his grandfather's lap.

Matty asked, "Pop Pop, tell me.
Is tonight the big night

When we drive to the airport
to meet Mommy's flight?"

Pop Pop smiled. "Yes, Dear! Later,
we'll go meet the plane,

And Mommy and Daddy will
be back home again."

POP

Then Nana came in, a large
plate in her hands,

Heaped with Christmas tree cookies—
My, how they looked grand.

With red and green sprinkles,
so sweet and enticing.

"Thanks, Nana!" said Matty. "Busken's
cookies with icing!"

Nana said, "Mom and Dad will
bring home your new sister,

From a faraway place, and
today we will meet her!

She'll enjoy growing up here.
Our city's unique.

Remember the great times we've
had this past week?

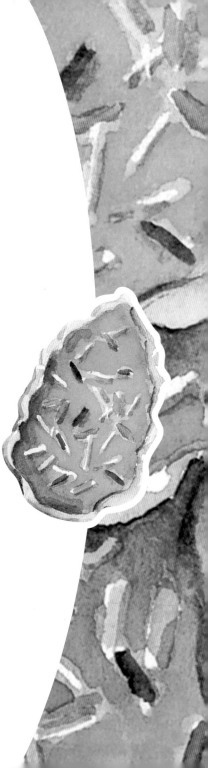

"Remember on Monday, we started our day,

By going downtown to the big train display?

Schoolchildren sang holiday
carols and songs.

We watched them, and listened,
and then sang along.

N S

"We saw Fountain Square's tall
Christmas tree, all aglow

Decorating the Square with
its sparkling red bows.

And Macy's big windows,
so festive and bright,

Snowflakes and garlands,
what a beautiful sight!

The ice rink was bustling and
teeming with skaters.

We sipped some hot cocoa, and
then walked to Graeter's."

FOUNTAIN SQUARE

"Yes!" Matty exclaimed. "Graeter's ice cream was nice.

All those yummy flavors— it's like paradise!

You got your favorite:
Black Raspberry Chip.

My Peppermint cone was a
ginormous dip!"

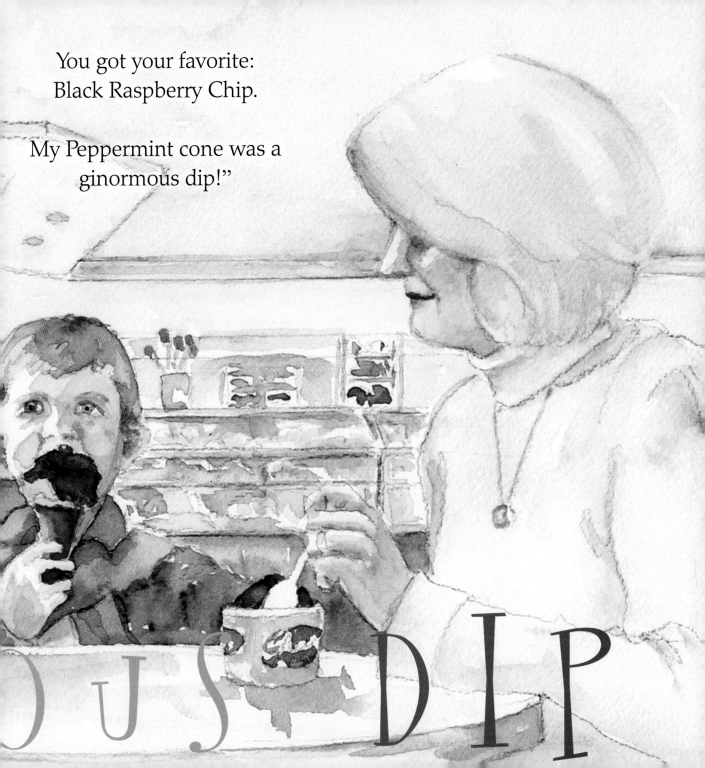

NUTCRAC

Nana said, "We saw one building,
lit up so bright,

Where the Nutcracker Ballet
was opening that night.

Your neighbor friend, Hannah,
is in it this year.

She's a tiny grey mouse.
How precious and dear!

The beautiful dancing is
always a thrill.

Someday I'll take you...
when you can sit still.

OHIO

"Then remember on Tuesday,
at Montgomery Inn?

You looked so cute with barbecue
sauce on your chin!

We sat watching the river,
and we felt so lucky,

Seeing barges and boats,
with a view of Kentucky.

The aroma of juicy plump
chicken and ribs...

How you cackled at us when
we tied on our bibs!

"Then, at the Zoo, on that crisp Wednesday night,

A magical place—The Festival of Lights!

You spied the big tunnel, all blinking and bright,

And ran right through the archway in joy and delight.

We saw tigers and gibbons and white polar bears;

The tuxedoed penguins looked so debonair!"

Pop Pop smiled, chiming in, "And then, back at home,

Nana ordered LaRosa's over the phone.

Matty remembered their number by heart:

347-1111! Boy, are you smart!

There's nothing like pizza to warm up the night,

And calzones and salad make dinner just right.

"Thursday, Union Terminal, our grand train station,

And Holiday Junction were our destination.

We saw model trains everywhere, all shapes and sizes,

You watched them, discovering lots of surprises!

You looked so grown up riding around on the train,

Clanging its brass bell again and again."

Nana laughed, "Yes, Thursday went by in a flash,

As off to get chili the three of us dashed.

We sat at the counter, got 3-Ways and Coneys,

And Matty piped up, 'I'd like cheese and spaghetti!'

Then I asked you, 'Please? Matty, what did you say?'

And you giggled, 'Oh, Nana! I want a 2-Way!' "

CHILI

Pop Pop said, "Now today, there's
one place left to visit,

Where we'll surely get into
the full Christmas spirit.

It's in Eden Park, at the
Krohn Conservatory.

The Nativity Crib tells the
whole Christmas story."

Donning scarves, hats, and gloves, they piled into the car,

And soon reached the log stable, under the stars.

A half-dozen sheep huddled close in the fold,

Their breath wispy clouds in the still, silent cold.

Matty listened, and heard the soft tinkling of bells,

And wrinkled his nose at the animal smells.

They tiptoed inside, stepping
out of the cold

And witnessed the tableau
so precious and old.

A cow softly mooing, a
donkey of grey,

Straw clung to their coats as
they munched on the hay.

They saw Mary and Joseph,
and in the starlight,

The sweet Baby Jesus, on the
first Christmas night.

Finally, the time they had waited for came:

It was time to meet Mommy and Daddy's airplane.

The air was as cold as an old Crosley 'fridge

As they drove o'er the river on the big Brent Spence Bridge.

At the airport, balloons were
a Christmassy sight.

Family and friends beamed
and laughed with delight!

From all around the Tri-State,
people had come

To meet Matty's sister and
bid her welcome.

At last, there they were, coming
straight down the hall.

His Mommy was smiling. His
Dad seemed so tall.

They hugged him hello, saying,
"We missed you, Matty!"

And there, in the car seat, was
his new sister, Annie.

ANN

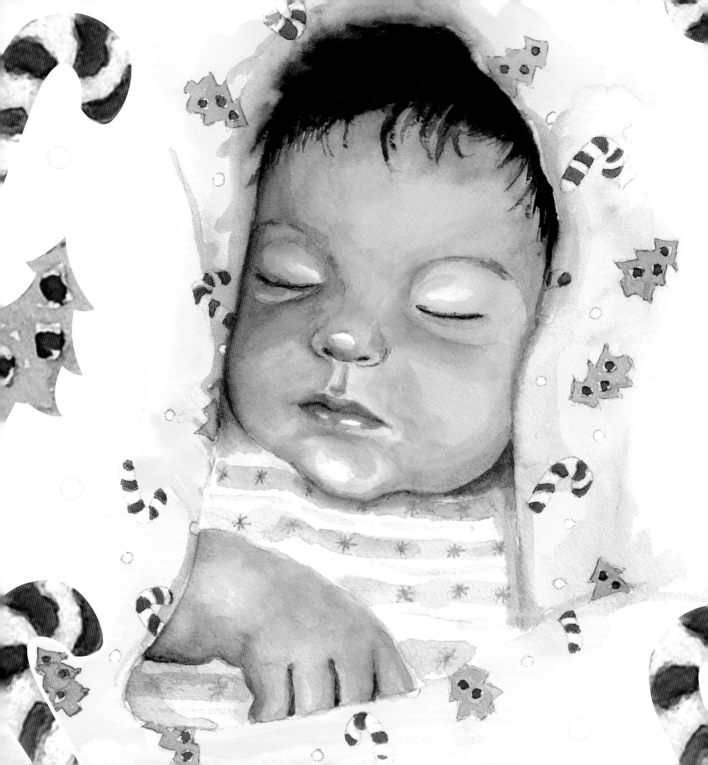

Sister's hair was so dark and her face was so round,

She was snug in a blanket, not making a sound.

Matty kissed her cheek gently, and touched her sweet ear,

And he whispered, "Hi Annie! I'm so glad you're here!"

Well, after that, everyone wanted a peek

At that fuzzy black head and that soft downy cheek.

It was loud as a Bengals game, or Reds baseball,

And bless baby Annie; she slept through it all.

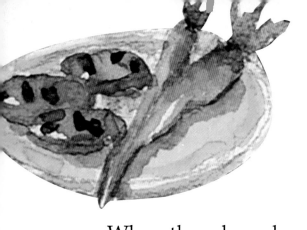

When they drove home, their neighborhood
sparkled with light.

Nana said, "Cincinnati sure does Christmas right!"

Matty left carrots for Santa's reindeer,

And cookies for Santa: "I know he'll be here!"

Then Nana kissed Matty under green mistletoe.

Pop Pop hugged him. "Night-night!
Time for bed. Up you go!"

NIGHT

NIGHT

Matty put on his jammies
and knelt down to pray,

Whispering, "Thank you, dear
God, for Jesus' birthday.

Thanks for Nana and Pop Pop,
and the fun that we had.

Bless my sister, Annie, and
my Mom and Dad.

Bless Bootsy, my bunny,
and Nuxie, my guppy,

And Kunzel, my kitty, and
Petey, my puppy.

And thank you for Annie.
I'm happy and glad!

She's the best Christmas
present that I ever had!"

Mommy and Daddy tucked
him snug into bed,

As visions of riverboats
danced in his head.

Santa and his reindeer soon
came from above,

And brought lots of toys to
that home filled with love.

And so ends our tale of a
young boy named Matty,

On the night before Christmas
here in Cincinnati.

"How we praise God, the Father of our Lord Jesus Christ, who has blessed us with every spiritual blessing in the heavenly realms because we belong to Christ. Long ago, even before he made the world, God loved us and chose us in Christ to be holy and without fault in his eyes. His unchanging plan has always been to adopt us into his own family by bringing us to himself through Jesus Christ. And this gave him great pleasure. So we praise God for the wonderful kindness he has poured out on us because we belong to his dearly loved Son."
—Ephesians 1:3-6; New Living Translation

To our readers:

We are adopted Cincinnatians. Neither of us was born or raised here. But as we've each measured our lives in muddy soccer shoes, carpools, trips to the vet, Friday night football games, and Opening Days, Cincinnati has woven its charms deeply into our hearts. This is our adopted city.

Likewise, Baby Annie is adopted, but in a more significant way. Her parents give her their last name, and she gains legal rights and privileges as their daughter. They love her deeply and passionately, just as they love Matty. And they will do their best to raise them both, making decisions based on the best information they have at the time. But they will never be perfect parents. After all, they are only human beings.

As believers in Jesus Christ, however, we have the perfect parent: God, our Father. We have been adopted into God's family, and have rights and privileges as His children. Our Father loves us perfectly, and unconditionally. He gives us what we need. We can go to Him with our troubles any time, and He'll always be there for us; He's never moody, petulant, or too busy. We can be confident that no matter what's happening in our lives, and in the world, He's always aware of everything, cares about all of it, and weaves it into the tapestry of time for our ultimate good. He knows us better than we know ourselves. If He corrects our behavior, we can be sure it's for a good reason. He gives us the certainty of a future with Him in heaven. He is a parent who always keeps His promises to his kids. Praise God for His goodness and grace, given to us, His adopted children through Christ.

—*Nadine and Marilyn*

Acknowledgements

This seemingly simple little book involved almost as many people as a Pops concert! We are deeply grateful to the following people for making it a reality:

- Carolyn Bond, Lisa Cadora, Sean Cahill, Peter Huffman, Rebecca Huffman, and Mary Pommert for reviewing the text and for their helpful feedback.
- Lisa Huffman for scene illustration photography on a very cold winter day.
- Courtney Laginess at Keating, Muething, and Klekamp, as well as Jim Singler, Laura Cox, and Stephanie Alexander, for guiding us through the intellectual property maze and for helping to structure our business in a way that's consistent with our objectives.
- Jim Swisher, Carol Miller, and Bruce Berno for their sage financial advice.
- Linda Ault, Cheri Brinkman, Jane Fischer, Damon Gray, Karen Kratz, Nydia Tranter, John Wenstrup, and Sr. Margie Efkeman, OSU, as well as all our friends, for their support and encouragement.
- Stuart Dornette, Katie Blackburn, Nancy Wygand, Nikki Hart, Patti Willis, Lori Fierro, Dan Busken, Allie Dobson, Lee Stautberg, Rich Graeter, Steven Schuckman, Mike LaRosa, Julie Strider, Holly Thomas, Jim Marx, Teena Schweier, Megan Pearce, Missy Knight, Christine Engels, Mike Laatsch, Chad Yelton, Brunhilde Kunzel, Lauren Roberson, Evan Andrews, Melissa Stormer, Allie Schroeder, Kate Smith, and Donzetta, Phil, Kim, and Bonnie Nuxhall, who assisted us in securing permission for references.
- Sharon Siepel and Mary-Cabrini Durkin for publishing industry insights.
- Stephanie Porter for incredibly helpful marketing comments and advice.
- Sara Hobson for meticulous and wise copy editing and proofing.
- Ken Riddiough for patiently developing our websites.
- Kristin Baker-Moser for author and illustrator photographs.
- Chad DeBoard for his wonderful design and production expertise, as well as Sarah Hawley, Janice Ellis, and all the staff at Orange Frazer Press.
- Will Saxby, as well as Tom and Marty Ferone, for modeling the illustrations.
- Dan and Amy Saxby, and their beautiful family, for inspiring the story.
- Laura Pulfer, Tricia Macke, and dede Muñoz for their kind reviews.

Special thanks and heartfelt appreciation to Marcy Hawley at Orange Frazer Press, and our dear friend Kathleen Cahall, who championed this project and mentored us from its inception. We couldn't have done it without you.

Finally, we thank our families, especially our husbands Mark and Brett, whose unconditional love and support helped us persevere, and our Sovereign Lord, who made it all possible.

Author & Illustrator

Both the Huffman and Lebhar families consider Cincinnati their home. Author Nadine Woodard Huffman and her husband, Mark, moved to the Queen City in 1984. They treasure holiday memories with their two daughters and son. Illustrator Marilyn M. Lebhar and her husband, Brett, came to Cincinnati in 1990. They celebrate Christmas with their two grown sons and daughter-in-law. The Huffmans and Lebhars live in Anderson Township.

Nadine Woodard Huffman

Marilyn M. Lebhar